40 PRAYERS
FOR ALL-AGE WORSHIP

40 PRAYERS

FOR ALL-AGE WORSHIP

Prayers for your
Church or small group

DAVID CLOWES

transforming lives together

40 PRAYERS FOR ALL-AGE WORSHIP
Published by David C Cook
4050 Lee Vance Drive
Colorado Springs, CO 80918 U.S.A.

Integrity Music Limited, a Division of David C Cook
Brighton, East Sussex BN1 2RE, England

The graphic circle C logo is a registered trademark of David C Cook.

All rights reserved. Except for brief excerpts for review purposes,
no part of this book may be reproduced or used in any form
without written permission from the publisher.

The website addresses recommended throughout this book
are offered as a resource to you. These websites are not
intended in any way to be or imply an endorsement on the
part of David C Cook, nor do we vouch for their content.

ISBN 978-0-8307-8232-1
eISBN 978-0-8307-8240-6

© 2020 David Clowes

The Team: Ian Matthews, Jack Campbell,
Jo Stockdale, Susan Murdock
Cover Design: Pete Barnsley

Printed in the United Kingdom
First Edition 2020

1 2 3 4 5 6 7 8 9 10

090120

CONTENTS

Introduction 7

Prayers of Praise 9

Prayers of Thanksgiving 21

Prayers of Confession 28

Bible Characters 32

Prayers for Others 49

About the Author 55

INTRODUCTION

Having published *500 Prayers for All Occasions* and *500 More Prayers for All Occasions* I was asked to develop a new series of books of prayer for use in small groups or in the home.

There are at least forty prayers in each of these books based around a single theme. Most of the content comes from my first two books of prayer for public worship, but has been revised and re-worked to make it appropriate for use in churches, small groups, the family situation, or for personal quiet time devotions.

My church background was firmly in the camp of extemporary prayer. I started to write my prayers down due to nervousness and on the advice of my preaching mentor who insisted on careful preparation not only of the hymns, readings, and sermon, but also of the prayers. I have long since realised the value of having a resource to be used as a flexible launch pad for my own prayer life which I could use and adapt as I wished.

I hope that is how you will approach these simple aids to prayer. They have been deliberately written in an uncomplicated style and with language that seeks to illuminate the joy of prayer. I have also tried to ensure that they are written in the language we use in our daily conversations. The aim of this is designed to make them easier to 'pray' and not simply to 'read'.

David Clowes
Stockport, April 2020

PRAYERS OF PRAISE

THE CALENDAR

Lord, we praise you for the calendars that hang on our walls;
for their pictures of birds and animals;
of people and places; of sea and sky.
They remind us each day of the good things
with which you have filled your world
and which you require us to protect.

Lord, we praise you for the calendars that hang on our walls;
for the months and the weeks; the days and the hours;
for the minutes and seconds.
They are waiting and ready to be used for the glory of
  your name
so that the whole world may know that Jesus is Lord.

Lord, we praise you for the calendars that hang on our walls;
for the time you have given to us
to give and to share, to love and to care, to offer peace
  and forgiveness.
It was your plan from the beginning
that no one be forgotten and peace be restored.

Lord, we praise you for the calendars that hang on our walls;
for the promise of hope that each new day brings
and for the new things we can learn before tomorrow begins;
for the fresh adventure of faith, of which each dawn is
   the herald.
May we so use each new day that tomorrow, for someone,
will be flooded with the joy of your love.

Lord, we praise you for the calendars that hang on our walls;
for the comfort we can offer to those whose days overflow
   with tears;
for the help we can give to those who feel lost and alone;
for the peace we can share with those whose hopes
   are broken.
May we so live that everyone we meet feels the presence of
   your grace
and the power of your love.

Lord, we praise you for the calendars that hang on our walls;
for the times we have been given to share your good news;
to make sure this day doesn't end before
we have spoken to someone of that love which never ends;
to take every opportunity to name Jesus as Lord.
May all we say and do this day
bring peace to our world and hope to our neighbour.

Lord, we praise you for the calendars that hang on our walls;
for they are like life—they have a start and a finish,
a beginning and an end;

they have a plan and a purpose and give direction to
   our days;
they announce a journey we must make and a goal
   to be reached.
Each day you give us another twenty-four hours
to be used to the full and lived for our Lord.

As we look at the calendar that hangs on our wall,
help us to begin each new day
walking in faith, putting our trust in you, Lord,
that, by your grace, we may give you
all the thanks and praise that you deserve. **Amen.**

BREAD OF HEAVEN

Bread, Lord—it's such ordinary stuff, and not a very
   exciting word.

For many people bread means money
and for most of us it's what we make our toast with.
It's ordinary stuff, for everyday people,
but daily bread was the first request in the prayer that Jesus
   gave us.
Lord, we thank you for the farmer who sows and reaps;
for the baker who mixes the dough and bakes the loaves;
for those who wrap it and bring it to our table.
Lord, we praise you for Jesus, our daily bread,
who offers us a life of challenge and adventure.
He promises to all who will listen to him
forgiveness and love beyond our deserving.

Lord Jesus, be like bread for us,
filling our hearts and our minds with the love of your Father.
Amen.

CREATION

Lord, you give us times of stillness
and quiet moments of life to remember you and your love.
We give you thanks
and we sing your praise.

Lord, you made the rippling streams and the mighty
   waterfalls
as signs of your goodness and power.
We give you thanks
and we sing your praise.

Lord, you built the snowy mountaintops and designed lakes
   of clear water
that fill us with hope and joy.
We give you thanks
and we sing your praise.

Lord, you created animals of every shape and size and colour
as well as birds and fish and insects.
We give you thanks
and we sing your praise.

Lord, your creation reflects your beauty and your glory;
it makes us want to worship you and to praise your name.

We give you thanks
and we sing your praise.

Lord, you gave us eyes to see and ears to hear,
lives to enjoy your creation, and voices to give you glory.
We give you thanks
and we sing your praise.

Lord, long ago you created glaciers that remind us
that you are the God who has no beginning and no end.
We give you thanks
and we sing your praise.

Lord, you gave us mighty rushing waters
that speak to us of your life-sustaining power and love.
We give you thanks
and we sing your praise.

Lord, the light sparkling on the water and sunsets that take
our breath away
speak to us of the light of the world.
We give you thanks
and we sing your praise.

In Jesus' name. **Amen.**

WE CAN SING AND WE CAN SHOUT!

Lord, we are so glad that you gave us our voices
and that we can use them to make so much noise—
we can sing and we can shout!

We can use our voices
to say please and to say thank you;
to say something kind to those who are sad;
to give encouragement to those who are hurting inside;
to show the way when someone is lost;
to say something good when others are being nasty;
to speak about Jesus, even when others only laugh.

We can use our voices
to sing your praise;
to say our prayers;
to speak of your love;
to shout aloud that we think you're wonderful.

We can make sure our voices keep quiet
instead of saying something hurtful or unkind;
we can be silent, instead of getting angry;
gentle instead of being a bully;
thoughtful instead of being selfish.

We can use our voices to say thank you for all the wonderful things
with which you fill our lives, our world, and our days;
to say sorry when what we say or do hurts you, other people, and ourselves;
to shout aloud that we follow Jesus and that we are giving our lives to him
whose life, death, and resurrection shout aloud your love for all the world.

Lord, we can sing and we can shout;
help us to sing and shout for Jesus. **Amen.**

MOTHERING SUNDAY

For our homes and our families
where we feel safe, loved, and wanted,
we praise you, Lord,
and we give you our thanks.

For our parents who love us and care for us
and through whom you gave us life,
we praise you, Lord,
and we give you our thanks.

For those who comfort us when we are afraid
and hold us when we are sad,
we praise you, Lord,
and we give you our thanks.

For those who are patient with us when we do wrong
and who care for us when we are ill,
we praise you, Lord,
and we give you our thanks.

For those we can trust and we know really love us
and for those who teach us to put our trust in you,
we praise you, Lord,
and we give you our thanks.

For aunts and uncles, for grandparents and cousins,
for all those who help us to know we belong,
we praise you, Lord,
and we give you our thanks.

For those who adopted or fostered us
and those who taught us to love and to give,
we praise you, Lord,
and we give you our thanks.

On this Mothering Sunday
we thank the Lord for our place in his family
and that he died on the cross to show us his love.
We praise you, Lord,
and we give you our thanks.

In the name of Jesus,
our brother and our friend. **Amen.**

GOD'S LOVE

Lord, you said God loves everyone;
there is not one person in the whole wide world that he doesn't love.
We suppose that means that you love even us;
that you love us when we are good and when we are not;
that you love us when we are happy and when we are sad;
that you love us when we are kind and when we hurt others;
that you love us when we forgive others and when we don't.
But, Lord, we know that your love means

that you love those we find hardest to like
and those who are unkind to us and have hurt us the most.
Lord, you have promised that when we put our trust in Jesus
there will never, ever be an end to your love for all eternity.
Amen.

OUR SPECIAL FRIEND

Lord, you are so amazing!
You are our special friend.
Lots of people promise to help us
and tell us they will never let us down.

But you are our special friend.
You died on the cross
that we might know our heavenly Father
and rose again as our precious living friend.

When we are lonely you promise to be with us,
even when we are at school or doing our homework.
When we are difficult and we want our own way
you are patient with us.
When we are hurting inside because of what other people
   say or do
you are gentle with us.

When we feel like jumping for joy
or want to hide ourselves away in a corner;
when we feel sad or afraid or full of excitement;
you share everything with us.
You are our living Lord and our special friend.

Lord, you are our special friend who never lets us down
but guides us in the way you want us to live.
Help us to give you the thanks and praise that you
   really deserve.

Lord, we are sorry for the times we have let you down,
for the ways we have hurt one another,
and for the chances we have missed to show your love
   and care.

Forgive us and, by your Holy Spirit,
help us to know the joy of beginning again.

We ask this in the name of Jesus, our friend and Lord.
   Amen.

CHILDREN'S LITANY OF PRAISE

We can dance and we can sing;
we give thanks to God
and we give him praise.

We can laugh and we can cry;
we give thanks to God
and we give him praise.

We can learn and we can play;
we give thanks to God
and we give him praise.

We can run and we can rest;
we give thanks to God
and we give him praise.

We can give and we can share;
we give thanks to God
and we give him praise.

For the food we eat and the strength it gives,
we give thanks to God
and we give him praise.

For games to play and friends to play with,
we give thanks to God
and we give him praise.

For songs to sing and praise to give,
we give thanks to God
and we give him praise.

For God's forgiveness even when we are wrong,
that he loves us and helps us begin again,
we give thanks to God
and we give him praise.

In Jesus' name. **Amen.**

LORD, SO GREAT

Lord, so great, you made the world.
Lord, so big, you hold it day by day.
Lord, so good, you gave us life.
Lord, so loving, you gave us Jesus.
Lord, so forgiving, you help us to start again.
Lord, so great, you help scientists to make discoveries that will change our lives,
Lord, so big, you call us to care for your world.
Lord, so good, you teach us to care for one another.
Lord, so loving, help us to show the love of Jesus each day.
Lord, so forgiving, help us to forgive one another,
knowing that we have been forgiven. **Amen.**

PRAYERS OF THANKSGIVING

THE DIFFERENCE

I am so small and you are so great.
Thank you, God.
Thank you, God.

I am so weak and you are so strong.
Thank you, God.
Thank you, God.

I can do so little and you can do everything.
Thank you, God.
Thank you, God.

I need others to help and you are the one who helps everybody.
Thank you, God.
Thank you, God.

I have a birthday each year to remember the day I was born,
but you are so great and so wonderful you have no
   beginning
and your love never ends.
Thank you, God.
Thank you, God.

I know so little about so many things,
but you know everything that there is to know about all
   things!
Thank you, God.
Thank you, God.

I am so small that grown-ups don't see me,
but you see everyone, everywhere, and for ever.
Thank you, God.
Thank you, God.

Thank you, Lord, for being so different and for loving us all
so much.
Thank you, God.
Thank you, God. Amen.

EDUCATION SUNDAY

We thank you for the world in which we live
which is full of so many good and exciting things
that we can learn and discover.
We thank you, Lord.
We thank you, Lord.

We thank you for our teachers at school
who help us to learn the things we need to know.
We thank you, Lord.
We thank you, Lord.

We thank you that Jesus was a teacher
to the disciples and to the crowds who listened to his stories.
We thank you, Lord.
We thank you, Lord.

We thank you for those who help us to learn about Jesus
and what it means to know him as Saviour and Lord.
We thank you, Lord.
We thank you, Lord.

We thank you for those who teach us to trust God
and show in their lives what it means to know Jesus.
We thank you, Lord.
We thank you, Lord.

Forgive us when we do not want to learn about you
and refuse to open our hearts and lives to your love.
We are sorry, Lord.
We are sorry, Lord.

Forgive us and teach us to be more forgiving
and more loving.
We ask this in Jesus' name. **Amen.**

BEGINNINGS

Lord, you were at the beginning of all things.
From you and by your sovereign power
everything we see had its beginning.
For the beginning of all good things,
we thank you, Lord.

Lord, you were there at our beginning.
You knew our names, even before we were born.
Every new step we take is already known to you.
For the beginning of all good things,
we thank you, Lord.

Lord, you have watched us as we have grown.
From our first day until the end of our days
our whole lives are held in your hands.
For the beginning of all good things,
we thank you, Lord.

Lord, every new skill we have learnt
and all the exciting discoveries we have made
were under your watchful eye.
Every good lesson we were taught
was dug from the quarry of your truth.
For the beginning of all good things,
we thank you, Lord.

Lord, you are at the start of every journey
and we find you waiting at our destination.
Your promise is to walk with us and to love us all our days.

For the beginning of all good things,
we thank you, Lord.

Lord, we thank you for every new friend we make
and those whose love and care make each day special,
and for those who show us the way
to become friends of Jesus.
For the beginning of all good things,
we thank you, Lord.

Lord, we thank you for each new flower
that adds colour and beauty to your wonderful world.
We praise you for the sun and the rain
that make things grow.
For the beginning of all good things,
we thank you, Lord.

Lord, we thank you for every new song
that points our thoughts and our praises to Jesus,
and we thank you for each time
we can meet together for worship.
For the beginning of all good things,
we thank you, Lord. Amen.

WE THANK YOU, LORD

For centuries and for decades; for days and for hours;
for every minute and each second
that come from your hand;
we praise your name
and we thank you, Lord.

For elephants, lions, and tigers; for kangaroos,
ostriches, and zebras;
for dogs and cats and rabbits and gerbils;
for every creature large and small;
we praise your name
and we thank you, Lord.

For tulips and daffodils; for chrysanthemums and roses;
for dandelions, buttercups, and daisies;
for every flower that adds colour to your world;
we praise your name
and we thank you, Lord.

For beech and elm; for oak and sycamore;
for pine, fir, and birch;
for the trees of the forest that come in all shapes and sizes;
we praise your name
and we thank you, Lord.

For grasshoppers and beetles; for bees and caterpillars;
for butterflies, dragonflies, and moths;
for tiny things that fly or crawl;
we praise your name
and we thank you, Lord.

For ducks and penguins; for sparrows and chaffinches;
for eagles, herons, and budgerigars;
for the songs they sing and the way they fly;
we praise your name
and we thank you, Lord.

For cornflakes and Rice Krispies; for biscuits and cakes;
for breakfast, lunch, and our evening meal;
for all the food we eat and for the strength it gives to us;
we praise your name
and we thank you, Lord.

For mothers and fathers; for brothers and sisters;
for aunties and uncles, and for relatives and friends;
for all the people we meet each day
at home, at school, at work, or at play;
we praise your name
and we thank you, Lord.

For your love that gave us life;
for your love in Jesus that gives us new life;
for your love that holds us and guards us each day;
for your love to us as Father, Son, and Holy Spirit;
we praise your name
and we thank you, Lord.

In Jesus' name. **Amen.**

PRAYERS OF CONFESSION

THE ENVIRONMENT

Lord, we thank you for giving us
such a wonderful world in which to live.
There is always so much to see, so much to do,
and so much to discover;
so many places to visit and so many people to meet.
You have made our lives so exciting
and each day is a new opportunity
to thank you and praise you
for all you have done and all you have given to us.
We thank you for Jesus, and that he came to show your love
for everyone, everywhere, and for ever.
Forgive us for being so selfish,
for not playing fair, and always wanting our own way;
for always wanting the best for ourselves
and not wanting the best for others too.
Forgive us and make us new, and make us more like Jesus.
In his name. **Amen.**

WE HAVE COME TO SAY

Lord, we have come to say we are sorry for the times
when we were angry;
when we wanted our own way;
when we said something that wasn't true;
when we didn't play fair;
when we didn't want to share;
when we were unkind, unhelpful, or selfish;
when we didn't want to say sorry.
Lord, we have come to say we are sorry
and to ask you not only to forgive us, but to help us
to be honest; to be caring;
to be helpful; to be loving;
to be forgiving;
so that the way we live will show that
Jesus lives in our hearts. **Amen.**

A CHILD'S CONFESSION

Lord, we are sorry for the wrong choices we make;
we are sorry that we are greedy and selfish;
we are sorry that we don't play fair and we cheat;
we are sorry that we like to get our own way.
Forgive us and help us to make a new start.
We ask this in Jesus' name. **Amen.**

ALL-AGE CONFESSION

For the wrong things we have said and done,
we have come to say
we are sorry, Lord.

For the times we have cheated and we have not played fair,
we have come to say
we are sorry, Lord.

For the times we have been selfish and wanted our own way,
we have come to say
we are sorry, Lord.

For the times we have not told the truth
and got others into trouble,
we have come to say
we are sorry, Lord.

For the times when our behaviour has hurt you
as we have spoilt things for other people and for ourselves,
we have come to say
we are sorry, Lord.

For the times we have forgotten to pray to you
and we have not made time to give you our worship,
we have come to say
we are sorry, Lord.

Quietly, in our own hearts, we will now tell God
the things for which we are sorry.

silence

Jesus died on the cross for us
and because we trust that you will forgive us

we have come to say
we are sorry, Lord. Amen.

MOTHERING SUNDAY

Lord, we confess that we have treated
those whom we should have cared for most
with an unkindness we would not have shown to strangers.
The way we speak to one another
and how we abuse our homes does not honour you.
Our selfish attitudes and our self-centred behaviour
do not allow others to see Christ in us.
Lord, forgive us and, by your Holy Spirit,
so renew our relationship with you
that those around us and those within our homes
may experience your love in their lives.
In Christ's name we pray. **Amen.**

LORD, WE NEED YOUR LIGHT

Lord, we confess that we need your light
to heal our brokenness;
to restore our relationships;
to show us the way;
to cleanse and renew us;
to enable us to offer forgiveness
to those who have hurt us most;
and to receive the forgiveness that you give
to those who come confessing their need of your light.
Lord, we confess our need of your light,
trusting that you will light up our lives with your grace. **Amen.**

BIBLE CHARACTERS

FOUR FISHERMEN

Lord, what did you see in them?
They were just four ordinary men;
they were simply fixing their fishing nets
and you just said, 'Come.'
Lord, what did you see in them?
They were not very clever;
they'd never been to school or passed an exam
and you just said, 'Come.'
Lord, what did you see in them? They were not very good
and they didn't have much time for you
and worship wasn't something that was high on their list.
But you just said, 'Come.'
Lord, what did you see in them—or in us?
Like those four fishermen we are not very good.
But though we are not special in the eyes of the world
you still call people like us to come follow Jesus
wherever he leads and wherever he goes. **Amen.**

THE WOMAN AT THE WELL

Lord, we don't know her name
and we don't know what she was like,

we don't know what she did
and we don't know if she had any family.
All we know is that she had made a mess of her life;
that was the woman at the well.
But, Lord, you seemed to know
absolutely everything about her.
You knew what she had done and how she had lived;
you knew she had no friends and that she trusted nobody;
you knew she was lonely and that she was hurting inside;
you knew just how much she wanted to begin again.
Lord, thank you for the story of the woman at the well.
We now know that, as with her,
you know everything in our hearts and in our lives;
you know the things that spoil our lives
and the good things that mean so much to us.
Lord, thank you for the promise that, like fresh spring water,
you are wanting to make our lives new;
to change who and what we are
and, by the Holy Spirit, to enable us to live the kinds of lives
that bring you thanks and praise.
Lord, fill us with your love, guide us by your Word,
and live in us—that we may have life that is real. **Amen.**

NICODEMUS—THE MAN WITH MUCH TO LEARN

Lord, the story of Nicodemus is so amazing.
He was a very religious person:
he certainly believed in God;
he said his prayers and read his Bible.

But he still had so much to learn about what it means
to become one of your children and part of your family.
He was so shocked when Jesus told him that
if he wanted to become a child of God
then his life needed to be changed so completely
and in such a dramatic way
that being 'born again' was the only way
it could be described.
Lord, it isn't just Nicodemus who has much to learn!
We want you to show us
not only how much you love each and every one of us
but also just how much you want to change every part of our lives.
It is only when we allow you to make us new
that we will really know, as if for the very first time,
what it means to call you 'our Father'.
Lord, touch our lives and make us new;
touch our hearts and make us your own;
touch our voices that we may give you
the thanks and praise that you deserve. **Amen.**

ELIJAH—THE MAN WHO STOOD FIRM

Lord, we want to praise you for all those
who have faced great opposition but stood firm for you;
for those who felt rejected and unwanted
but were faithful to you.
We want to thank you for the stories about Elijah
and the way he was ready to challenge anyone and everyone
because of his faith in you.

We praise you for his willingness
to stand out from the crowd;
to be unpopular and to be ready for people to laugh at him
because he trusted in you.
We thank you for his example
of what it means to put you first
every day, in everything, and in every way.
Lord, we praise you because you are so great, so loving,
and so worthy of all that we can say and do in your name.
Help us never to be happy
just to sing your praise each Sunday
or to say a prayer when we are afraid.
Like Elijah, help us to allow nothing and no one
to prevent us living each day for the praise of your name.
We ask this for Jesus' sake. **Amen.**

MARY AND MARTHA—EXAMPLES TO LEARN FROM

Lord,
We thank you for Mary and Martha
and for the way, together, they show us how to follow Jesus.

Martha was the one who was always busy
and she wanted to make sure that Jesus felt welcome.
She was never still, always on the go—
never a moment just to be with Jesus.

Mary wanted to spend her time sitting at Jesus' feet
and enjoying simply being with him.

She spent her time listening to the things he said
but she was in danger of not putting them into action.

Sometimes we are like Martha
who was trying to impress Jesus
and we forget to make time to talk to him in prayer.
Other times we are like Mary,
our focus is on being with Jesus
and we easily forget to be ready to serve in his name.

So, Lord, help us to be a little bit like Martha,
ready for action when Jesus calls us;
and remind us, like Mary, that you are calling us to serve you
but we will miss hearing your voice, if we don't listen.
We ask this in Jesus' name. **Amen.**

MOSES AND ME

I've been thinking, Lord, about Moses and me.
Like me, you gave him life and people who cared about him.
Though he lived in a palace and had more good things
than he really deserved,
he never forgot his people and their needs.

I've been thinking, Lord, about Moses and me.
Like me, he could be strong; he could also be weak;
he did some good things and things he knew were wrong.
But he always trusted your love for him.

I've been thinking, Lord, about Moses and me.
Like Moses, each day you are calling me

to trust you, to serve you, to praise you,
and to do what you want me to do with my life.
Lord, I want to praise you for all the love and care
that I receive each day.
I want to thank you that you love me when I'm good
and when I'm not.
I want to say yes when you ask me
to give, to love, and to share.
Walk with me, Lord, so that I can hold your hand
and follow the path through life you have chosen for me.
Amen.

THE PRODIGAL COMES HOME

Lord, we know the story of the prodigal son,
the young man who made a mess of his life.
He thought of nothing and no one except himself
and what he wanted.
He was greedy, selfish, and rude, and he didn't seem to care
who got hurt by his selfishness
or what it cost to clear up the damage his greed had caused.
If he were alive today we would have called him a vandal,
he would have been in trouble with the police
and have been given an ASBO.
Yet we thank you, Lord, that this story has a great ending
for the awful young man.
He allowed God to change his heart
and to transform his attitude
to himself, to other people, and to what really matters in life.
We thank you for the story

of his welcome home by his father
and for the way it reminds us that each of us
can know you as Father.
We praise you that no matter
what we have done or failed to do
and no matter how far we have wandered away from you,
your incredible love reaches out and changes the way we live.
You draw us to yourself and, even though we don't deserve it,
you welcome us home,
and you do it for the sake of your Son,
in whose name we ask our prayer. **Amen.**

ISAIAH'S BIG DAY

Lord, you gave me such a surprise!
It was that day when you spoke to me in your temple.
I had been there many, many times before
but I had never, ever heard your voice as I did that day.
I have offered you prayers of thanks and sung songs of praise
but I had never even stopped to think
that you might have been there—
listening and enjoying it all!
I had read your Word
and listened to those who seemed to know what it meant.
But I never knew you wanted me to listen to you
and that through your Word
you were wanting to speak to me.
But now, Lord, everything has changed—
all because of that day in your house.
It was then that I did hear you speak—

and I knew that you were speaking to me.
Now I hear you speaking everywhere and through everyone.
I hear your voice in the most surprising places
and through the most unexpected people.
You speak to me through those who know you
and through those who don't;
through those I like and through those I don't!
Now that I know you are always wanting to speak to me
it makes each day a day of discovery
and coming to worship is something
I really, really look forward to—
just because I am meeting with you.
Lord, I want to praise you for opening my mind,
my ears, and my eyes
to hear and to know you, here and everywhere.
I want to thank you for showing me that you do speak—
but that I will hear your voice only when you know that I
am ready to say,
'Yes, here I am, send me.' **Amen.**

PETER—THE MAN WHO WAS CHANGED

Lord, how did it happen?
How did Peter become the one who was your spokesperson?
If we remember correctly,
he was forever saying the wrong thing and letting you down.
He even denied that he ever knew you,
which must have really upset you.
We would never have forgiven him—
but you simply welcomed him back

as your friend and disciple
and even gave him the important job
of feeding your sheep—
caring for those who put their trust in you.
Lord, didn't Peter run away?
We know he ran to the tomb on Easter day,
but it wasn't Peter who found faith at that moment;
it was John who believed what he saw in the tomb.
But, come the day of Pentecost,
everything and everyone was changed.
When the Holy Spirit came
he overwhelmed them all—including Peter.
That's why he could stand up in front of them all
and tell all the people the truth,
that the Jesus who had died on the cross was alive again
and, through the Holy Spirit, helps us all to speak of him
and to live for him every day. **Amen.**

NOAH—THE MAN PEOPLE LAUGHED AT

Lord, we want to praise you for Noah
and for the way that he listened to you;
for the way he did what you wanted even when others
laughed at his plans.
Lord, we want to thank you for Noah, and how he never
gave up but trusted you even when it was very hard;
for the way he was willing to obey you when he had only
your word to trust.
Lord, we want to praise you
that you still want to speak to us today,

and we thank you that we can trust you completely
no matter what other people may say.
Lord, we thank you for Noah,
whose trust in your word was rewarded
by your love that was with him each day.
Like Noah we offer you our worship
and we bring our songs of thanks and praise. **Amen.**

SAMUEL—THE BOY WHO LISTENED

Lord, we thank you for the story of Samuel
and how he listened to your voice;
he believed that you were there
and he trusted that you would never leave him.
Lord, we praise you for showing us that though, like Samuel,
we may not be big and strong,
you still want to share our lives and to live in our hearts.
Lord, we thank you for the story of Samuel
and how he did what you told him to do;
that, though you are so very great
and a really wonderful God,
you have a place for everyone
in your amazing plan to show your love to all the world.
Lord, we praise you that you still speak today—
if not always in the same way that you spoke to Samuel.
You make your presence felt in our hearts and in our lives.
Lord, we thank you that you speak to us
through the things we see and through the things we hear;
through people we love and through those we trust.
Lord, we praise you for the way you make us uncomfortable

when we say or do the wrong thing,
and you fill us with a sense of fulfilment
when we sing your praise and read your Word.
Lord, we thank you for Jesus,
through whom you speak loud and clear.
Speak, Lord; we really want to know what you want us to do
and how you want us to live.
And speak to us through Jesus,
for his is the name we use when we speak to you. **Amen.**

GIDEON—AND HIS AMAZING DISCOVERY

Lord, you are amazing!
Every time we think we know who you are
and we think we know what you can do,
again and again you do the most amazing things.
Lord, Gideon discovered just how amazing you are.
He wasn't very brave, he wasn't very strong,
he wasn't very important,
and he didn't think you could use him.
But you amazed him by what you did.
Lord, we want to praise you for being
the really amazing God that you are;
that you are bigger than the greatest thing we can think of
and more wonderful than anything we have ever seen.
We praise you that, as with Gideon, you can and will use us
in ways that will take our breath away.
We bring our prayers in the name of Jesus,
the most amazing gift of all. **Amen.**

HEROES OF FAITH

Lord, did we hear you correctly?
For a moment we thought you were wanting us
to be heroes of faith.
But they were people who were special
and lived a long time ago;
they were empowered by the Holy Spirit
for the challenging tasks you had given them to do.
We remember their names on the roll call
of those who have done great things
and brought glory to your name.
We rejoice when we hear of Abraham and Moses,
of Joshua and King David, of Peter and Paul,
and of all those whose names the Bible records
as heroes of faith in the service of their Lord.
We thank you for your heroes in later history
who transformed your world:
those like Luther and Wilberforce, Pankhurst and Fry,
and in our own day, Mother Teresa and Nelson Mandela.
Lord, we know that you can't really mean it,
but it seems that you are calling ordinary people like us
to be your heroes of faith for the people we meet.
But perhaps, just perhaps, the heroes of the past
were ordinary like us
and they simply allowed you to do extraordinary things.
Lord, by your grace and through the power of your Spirit,
open our eyes—to see your glory;
open our minds—to discover your truth;
open our hearts—to receive your Spirit;
that you may do something unexpected even through us.
  Amen.

THE MAN WITH A DONKEY

Lord, we don't know who he was or what he did,
we don't even know what his name was—
he was just the man with a donkey.
We don't know if he was rich or if he was poor,
we don't know if he was old or if he was young—
all we know is that he was the man with a donkey.
We don't know how well he knew Jesus
or if he knew him at all.
We don't know if the request for his donkey
came as a big surprise
or if it had all been planned from the first.
But we do know he was the man with a donkey.
We thank you, Lord, for the man with a donkey
and that he lent it to Jesus on that Palm Sunday.
We thank you more that,
whoever we are and whatever we have,
you can still use us like the man with a donkey
in ways we never dreamt of
and for things that seem impossible.
What we have and what we are may not seem so much,
and others may think we are foolish
for even daring to hope that we might be useful to you.
But thank you, Lord, as with the man with a donkey,
that you have a purpose for us
and what we have now will be useful to you. **Amen.**

JOSHUA—THE MAN WHO STOOD FIRM

Lord, we want to thank you for the stories of Joshua.
He was a person with limitations just like us.
He didn't always find it easy to do what he knew was right
or to do what you wanted him to do.
Lord, we thank you that Joshua listened to your word
and was ready to trust you even when it was very hard.
You gave him the courage he needed to win the battle
against the temptation to give up and give in
and to serve you no matter what others said or did.
Lord, help us to be like Joshua,
that we might be able to stand firm, to stand out,
to stand for you. **Amen.**

JONAH—THE MAN WHO RAN AWAY

Lord, sometimes we feel sorry for Jonah.
He was just an ordinary little person
that you called to do something very special for you.
What we don't understand is why you called him
to do what he didn't want to do.
You knew he was all mixed up inside
and that he was full of wrong ideas and bad thoughts.
Lord, we praise you that your love is so very strong
that you call us to help and to care
even for those we don't like
and you expect us to forgive even those who are very unkind.
We thank you that, as with Jonah,
you are always wanting to help us
to see everything and everyone as you see them.

Help us to allow you to change the way we think,
to fill our lives with your love,
and to offer kindness and friendship to those who are lonely
and to those who feel they are not wanted,
and to do it in Jesus' name. **Amen.**

DANIEL—THE MAN WHO WAS BRAVE

Lord, we like Daniel because he always did what was right.
Daniel was special because he put you first in everything
and trusted you completely.
Lord, we like Daniel because he was so brave,
so strong, and so full of love for you.
Lord, we like Daniel because he told others about you
and helped them to know what a wonderful God you are.
He wanted everyone he met to trust you
and showed them all what it means to love you completely.
Lord, we like Daniel; help us to be like him. **Amen.**

BLIND BARTIMAEUS

Lord, sometimes everything seems to go wrong:
we think we have some really big problems
and we don't know what to do.
Lord, sometimes we feel afraid
and there is no one to help us.
We have so many questions and we can't find the answers.
Lord, Bartimaeus was blind
and that made life very hard for him.
He must have had lots of questions,

but when he called out to Jesus he found someone
to help, to listen, to heal,
and to answer his deepest questions.
Lord, though we can't see you,
we know that you are always with us.
Though we can't touch you, we know you are always ready
to answer our questions and to help us—
when, like Bartimaeus, we call out to you. **Amen.**

THE BOY WITH THE LOAVES AND THE FISHES

He was just a boy with some loaves and fishes.
He had probably come with his friends and family.
He had heard so much about Jesus
and he wanted to hear just one of his stories.
It had been a perfect day as they sat on the grass
and enjoyed simply being with him.
Kindness and joy were written all over Jesus' face;
what he said and what he did made God's presence so real.
You felt you could reach out and put your hand into God's,
knowing for certain his love had found you.
He was just a boy with some loaves and fishes.
To go on a picnic was nothing new
except that this day was different—he would never forget
how Jesus had fed the five thousand with his packed lunch.
Lord, we praise you for the story of the boy
with some loaves and some fishes.
Now we know that whatever
we have we can place into your hands

and watch you work another miracle
to bring hope, joy, and peace to your broken world.
Lord, whatever we have is what you have given
and what you have given is not ours to keep.
But once we place ourselves and our gifts into your hands,
it is then that you can work your miracle
of hope, joy, and healing. **Amen.**

PRAYERS FOR OTHERS

HANDS OF PRAYER

Cut out five large 'hands' with the words WORLD, CHURCH, PEOPLE, and OURSELVES on four of them, and one left blank for them to write the things or people they want to pray for. Younger children can colour them in during the first part of the service. They are then brought forward one by one as the following prayers are said, placing them on a prayer board.

WORLD

Lord, we pray for your world which you gave us to live in and to care for.
We pray for the people of [*name a current area of need*] and
   for [*name an area of conflict*],
that there will be peace, hope, and forgiveness.
This is our prayer.
We put our prayers in the hands of Jesus.

CHURCH

Lord, we pray for the church,
for those who belong to your family here
and all the other churches in this area.
We pray for their leaders and all their congregations.

We pray especially for [*name a local congregation*].
This is our prayer.
We put our prayers in the hands of Jesus.

PEOPLE

Lord, we pray for people.
We pray for those who give a helping hand to others;
for those who reach out to touch those whose lives are in a mess,
to hold those who are sad or in pain.
We pray for young people going to college or university and for [*name a local youth group*].
This is our prayer.
We put our prayers in the hands of Jesus.

OURSELVES

Lord, we pray for ourselves
and all that we will be facing this week;
for all the things that are making us happy or sad,
angry or full of joy.
We pray that we may know the peace and the hope
that comes from placing everything in our lives into your hands.
This is our prayer.
We put our prayers in the hands of Jesus.

In the quietness, we pray for anyone we know to be in need of God's peace, joy, healing power, and love.
This is our prayer.
We put our prayers in the hands of Jesus.

We ask all our prayers in the name of Jesus. **Amen.**

THINK OF SOMEONE

Think of someone at school, at work, or at home who is ill.
Ask God to be with them and their family.

Think of someone you know; a friend,
a member of your family,
or someone who lives down your road who is unhappy
or always on their own.
Ask that God will help them to know that he is there.

Think of someone who doesn't think that they
    matter anymore
or who feels that everything has gone wrong.
Ask God to show them how much they matter to him.

Think of someone who is really, really happy, someone who is
very excited, someone who has been given some good news.
Ask God to help them share their joy.

Think of someone at school, someone you know, a friend,
a member of your family
who doesn't come to church or Sunday school,
someone who doesn't know how much God loves them.
Ask God to fill them with his love.

Think of someone at home, at school,
or at work who is very frightened,
someone who does not know what to do,
what to say, or how to cope with what is making them afraid.
Ask God to give them courage.

Think of yourself and all the things
that you must do this week;
things you are looking forward to and things that you aren't,
things that make you unhappy or afraid
and things that make you excited.
Ask God to share everything, every day with you.

Lord, in your mercy,
hear our prayer. Amen.

THOSE IN NEED OF FRUITFULNESS

We pray for those in need of love,
for those whose lives have been spoilt by neglect,
and for those who never received love
that was unconditional.
May the Spirit's presence in their lives bear fruit in love.
This is our prayer.
We ask it in Jesus' name.

We pray for those in need of joy;
for those whose lives are empty or who live alone;
and for those filled with despair.
May the Spirit's presence in their lives bear fruit in joy.
This is our prayer.
We ask it in Jesus' name.

We pray for those who long for peace;
for those who have lost home and family
in earthquake, storm, or sickness

and for those who are longing to find peace.
May the Spirit's presence in their lives bear fruit in peace.
This is our prayer.
We ask it in Jesus' name.

We pray for those who are in need of patience;
for those whose impatience towards others and themselves
is the cause of hurt, pain, and spoilt lives.
May the Spirit's presence in their lives
bear fruit in patience.
This is our prayer.
We ask it in Jesus' name.

We pray for those whose kindness to ourselves and to others
has been a source of hope and encouragement;
for those whose caring, sensitive compassion
brings joy to the heart of God.
May the Spirit's presence in their lives bear fruit in kindness.
This is our prayer.
We ask it in Jesus' name.

We pray for those whose lives are examples of God's goodness;
for those whose words and deeds make Jesus real
as they show the love of God to those they meet.
May the Spirit's presence in their lives bear fruit in goodness.
This is our prayer.
We ask it in Jesus' name.

We pray for those whose faithfulness to Jesus
brings them rejection and opposition from others;

for those who are faithful in the service of Christ.
May the Spirit's presence in their lives
bear fruit in faithfulness.
This is our prayer.
We ask it in Jesus' name.

We pray for those whose gentleness
is the source of hope and encouragement for many;
for those whose gentleness sometimes makes them vulnerable.
May the Spirit's presence in their lives bear fruit in gentleness.
This is our prayer.
We ask it in Jesus' name.

We pray for those whose lives are the cause
of despair and heartache
for those who care about them;
for those who are finding self-control is only possible
when Jesus is Lord of their lives.
May the Spirit's presence in their lives bear fruit in self-control.
This is our prayer.
We ask it in Jesus' name.

In the name of Jesus and in the power of the Spirit. **Amen.**

ABOUT THE AUTHOR

David Clowes, born in Ellesmere Port, left school at fifteen following a secondary modern education. In 1965 he committed his life to Christ at Heaton Mersey Methodist and in 1967 he received God's call into the Methodist ministry. He trained at Hartley Victoria College and gained a degree in theology at the University of Manchester.

David served in a number of churches in the northwest of England before retiring in 2010 after thirty-five years in active ministry. His first book, *500 Prayers for All Occasions*, began as a spiritual exercise during a sabbatical. This was followed by *500 More Prayers for All Occasions*. His third book of prayers, *500 Prayers for the Christian Year*, is based on scriptures from the Revised Common Lectionary.

David is married to Angela, and they have two married sons, a foster son, and four grandchildren.